P9-DFT-015

Math Activities

This book belongs to

Malia Grace Walton

Friday

Going to the Zoo

To help the tiger find the way to its den, solve each problem.
Then go to **start** and color the boxes with even sums.

start

	8 + 2 = 10	6 + 6 = 12	4 + 4 = 8	5 + 8 = 13
	11 + 6 = 17	13 + 4 = 17	10 + 6 = 16	13 + 2 = 15

7 + 6 = 13	11 + 2 = 13	3 + 3 = 6	8 + 4 = 12	7 + 7 = 14	5 + 11 = 16	14 + 5 = 19
8 + 7 = 15	4 + 9 = 13	5 + 7 = 12	12 + 5 = 17	10 + 5 = 15	9 + 8 = 17	9 + 4 = 13
11 + 3 = 14	12 + 6 = 18	9 + 7 = 16	15 + 4 = 19	12 + 3 = 15	17 + 4 = 21	7 + 10 = 17
7 + 5 = 12	5 + 12 = 17	9 + 4 = 13	4 + 7 = 11	9 + 6 = 15	6 + 7 = 13	8 + 5 = 13
6 + 8 = 14	4 + 6 = 10	2 + 12 = 14	8 + 5 = 13	15 + 2 = 17		
15 + 2 = 17	7 + 8 = 15	5 + 9 = 14	4 + 8 = 12	6 + 8 = 14		

2

Odd or Even

Solve each problem. Draw a circle around each problem with an odd difference.

1. $\begin{array}{r} 15 \\ -\ 7 \\ \hline \end{array}$ 8 $\begin{array}{r} 21 \\ -\ 19 \\ \hline \end{array}$ $\begin{array}{r} 10 \\ -\ 6 \\ \hline \end{array}$ $\begin{array}{r} 12 \\ -\ 4 \\ \hline \end{array}$ $\begin{array}{r} 14 \\ -\ 2 \\ \hline \end{array}$ $\begin{array}{r} 10 \\ -\ 0 \\ \hline \end{array}$

2. $\begin{array}{r} 9 \\ -\ 7 \\ \hline \end{array}$ 2 $\begin{array}{r} 20 \\ -\ 14 \\ \hline \end{array}$ $\begin{array}{r} 15 \\ -\ 2 \\ \hline \end{array}$ $\begin{array}{r} 11 \\ -\ 6 \\ \hline \end{array}$ $\begin{array}{r} 19 \\ -\ 6 \\ \hline \end{array}$ $\begin{array}{r} 18 \\ -\ 4 \\ \hline \end{array}$

3. $\begin{array}{r} 19 \\ -\ 11 \\ \hline \end{array}$ $\begin{array}{r} 13 \\ -\ 6 \\ \hline \end{array}$ $\begin{array}{r} 16 \\ -\ 7 \\ \hline \end{array}$ $\begin{array}{r} 12 \\ -\ 9 \\ \hline \end{array}$ $\begin{array}{r} 20 \\ -\ 19 \\ \hline \end{array}$ $\begin{array}{r} 15 \\ -\ 8 \\ \hline \end{array}$

4. $\begin{array}{r} 17 \\ -\ 5 \\ \hline \end{array}$ $\begin{array}{r} 10 \\ -\ 8 \\ \hline \end{array}$ $\begin{array}{r} 9 \\ -\ 5 \\ \hline \end{array}$ $\begin{array}{r} 15 \\ -\ 9 \\ \hline \end{array}$ $\begin{array}{r} 11 \\ -\ 9 \\ \hline \end{array}$ $\begin{array}{r} 16 \\ -\ 2 \\ \hline \end{array}$

5. $\begin{array}{r} 10 \\ -\ 4 \\ \hline \end{array}$ $\begin{array}{r} 20 \\ -\ 0 \\ \hline \end{array}$ $\begin{array}{r} 17 \\ -\ 4 \\ \hline \end{array}$ $\begin{array}{r} 19 \\ -\ 11 \\ \hline \end{array}$

FS109045 • Math Activities

Animal Mystery

Write each sum. Then use the code to find the letter that goes with each sum. Write the letter in the circle.

1.

	+ 6	
4		◯
1		◯
6		◯
3		◯
7		◯

2.

	+ 4	
4		◯
3		◯
8		◯
4		◯
8		◯
1		◯
7		◯
0		◯
2		◯
9		◯

3.

	+ 7	
3		◯
4		◯
6		◯
7		◯

7	13	9	4	10	5	8	14	12	6	11
r	s	g	l	f	d	c	h	o	e	i

FS109045 • Math Activities

Sweet Families

Read each riddle and complete each fact family. Write four
number sentences for each fact family.

1. I'm the smallest
   number in
   my family.
   The other two
   numbers are
   13 and 9. What
   number am I?

   ___ + ___ = ___

   ___ + ___ = ___

   ___ − ___ = ___

   ___ − ___ = ___

   ___

3. I'm the biggest
   number in
   my family.
   The other two
   numbers are
   3 and 9. What
   number am I?

   ___ + ___ = ___

   ___ + ___ = ___

   ___ − ___ = ___

   ___ − ___ = ___

   ___

2. I'm not the
   biggest or the
   smallest number
   in my family.
   The other two
   numbers are 7
   and 15. What
   number am I?

   ___ + ___ = ___

   ___ + ___ = ___

   ___ − ___ = ___

   ___ − ___ = ___

   ___

4. I'm not the
   biggest or the
   smallest number
   in my family.
   The other two
   numbers are
   3 and 9. What
   number am I?

   ___ + ___ = ___

   ___ + ___ = ___

   ___ − ___ = ___

   ___ − ___ = ___

   ___

FS109045 • Math Activities

That's Fishy

Find the sum of the numbers on each fish. Then cross out the fish in each row that does not belong.

1.

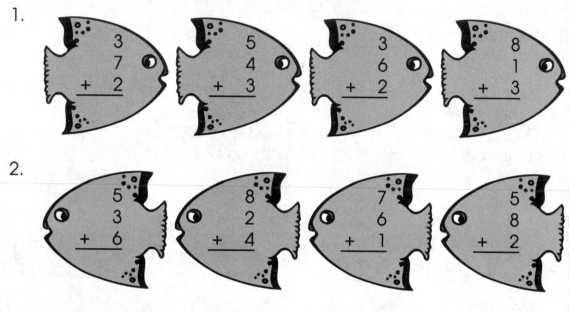

Row 1 fish:
- $3 + 7 + 2$
- $5 + 4 + 3$
- $3 + 6 + 2$
- $8 + 1 + 3$

2.

Row 2 fish:
- $5 + 3 + 6$
- $8 + 2 + 4$
- $7 + 6 + 1$
- $5 + 8 + 2$

3.

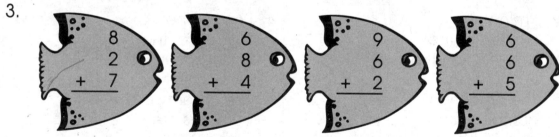

Row 3 fish:
- $8 + 2 + 7$
- $6 + 8 + 4$
- $9 + 6 + 2$
- $6 + 6 + 5$

4.

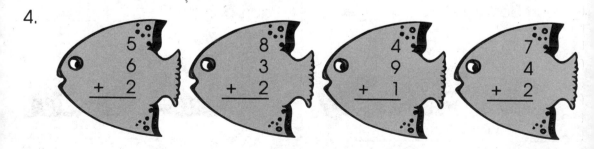

Row 4 fish:
- $5 + 6 + 2$
- $8 + 3 + 2$
- $4 + 9 + 1$
- $7 + 4 + 2$

FS109045 • Math Activities

Seal Squares

Complete each magic square with the numbers on the ball.
The sum of each row, column, and diagonal should match the
number on the seal.

Reptile Problems

Solve each problem.

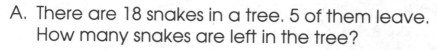

A. There are 18 snakes in a tree. 5 of them leave.
   How many snakes are left in the tree?

   _____ snakes

B. There are 9 turtles in a row. When the rest are
   sleeping, 6 of them go. How many are left?
   Do you know?

   _____ sleeping turtles

C. There are 8 lizards on a rock. Then 9 more
   come out of a sock. How many lizards are out
   on the rock?

   _____ in all

D. There are 4 hungry alligators searching for
   some lunch. They find 12 big fish to munch!
   How many alligators and fish?

   _____ in all

FS109045 • Math Activities

Animal Problems

Solve each problem.

There are 10 sweet birds singing in their nest. 2 decide to take a little rest. How many are still singing their best?

_____ birds

There are 13 kangaroos bouncing in the sun. 7 more come to join the fun. How many are on the run?

_____ kangaroos

There are 13 monkeys swinging in the trees. Suddenly, 4 of them land on their knees. How many monkeys are still swinging?

_____ monkeys

There are 6 little bear cubs sitting in a row. Then they see 7 more cubs below. How many bears are there in all, do you know?

_____ bear cubs

There are 14 leopards with lots of spots. 11 of them have tails with knots! How many leopard tails do not have knots?

_____ leopard tails

Write your own animal problem and solve it.

FS109045 • Math Activities

Leaping Lions

At the Lion Show, lions jump through hoops to score points. The lion with the most points wins.

Complete the score card below. Write each number to determine the winner.

	Hundreds	Tens	Ones	Score
Frisky	2	3	7	
Rex	3	4	5	
Whiskers	4	3	0	
Scratch	3	8	3	
Claude	2	0	4	

First place goes to _____.

Second place goes to _____.

Third place goes to _____.

Fourth place goes to _____.

Fifth place goes to _____.

A Spotted Fellow

Find the place value of 5 in each number. Use the chart to color the spots.

Place Value	Color
Ones	Green
Tens	Purple
Hundreds	Blue
Thousands	Red

5
95
51
57
151
45
54
15
175
562
58
517
95
59
5,787
154
735
75
53
85
45
52
5,072
35
115
345
3,952
2,530
511
352
5,273
915
65
50
56
25
5

© Carson-Dellosa   FS109045 • Math Activities

Snake Sequence

Fill in each blank below with the number that comes before, between, or after.

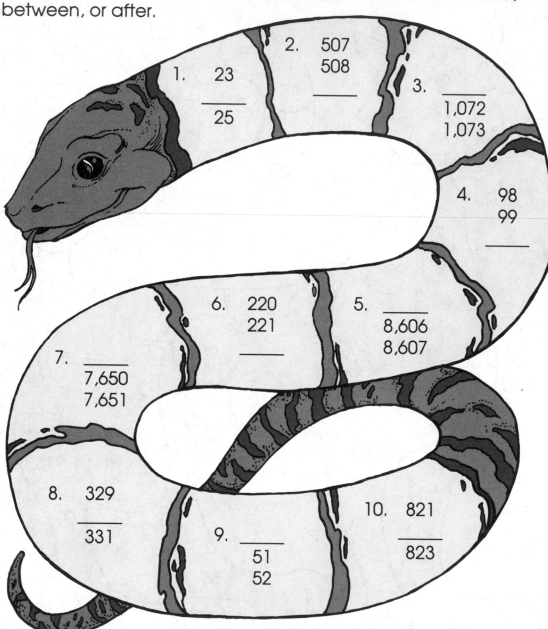

1. 23
   ___
   25

2. 507
   508
   ___

3. ___
   1,072
   1,073

4. 98
   99
   ___

5. ___
   8,606
   8,607

6. 220
   221
   ___

7. ___
   7,650
   7,651

8. 329
   ___
   331

9. ___
   51
   52

10. 821
    ___
    823

FS109045 • Math Activities

Sorting It Out

Use the diagram to answer the questions below.

Reptiles   Animals with
                                                     Stripes

A. How many reptiles are shown? _____

B. How many animals with stripes are shown? _____

C. Which animal is a reptile that also has stripes? _____

D. How many more animals are reptiles than are not reptiles?

_____

E. Name the animals that have stripes. _____

_____

F. Name the animals that are reptiles. _____

_____

Comparing Pairs

Compare the numbers. Write >, <, or = in each circle.

1. 472 ◯ 463   107 ◯ 170   297 ◯ 397

2. 504 ◯ 405   767 ◯ 676   976 ◯ 484

3. 334 ◯ 337   373 ◯ 373   39 ◯ 46

4. 762 ◯ 752   109 ◯ 104   930 ◯ 910

5. 389 ◯ 689   681 ◯ 861   414 ◯ 414

          FS109045 • Math Activities

More Pairs

Compare the numbers. Write >, <, or = in each circle.

1. 115 ◯ 115   1,203 ◯ 1,203   105 ◯ 115

2. 41 ◯ 41   2,232 ◯ 2,742   2,899 ◯ 1,001

3. 5,209 ◯ 5,466   69 ◯ 39   3,257 ◯ 3,257

4. 67 ◯ 67   784 ◯ 784   38 ◯ 42

5. 705 ◯ 486   600 ◯ 599   716 ◯ 800

6. 57 ◯ 28   310 ◯ 310   80 ◯ 108

7. 53 ◯ 53   367 ◯ 376   120 ◯ 12

8. 500 ◯ 5,000   19 ◯ 205   800 ◯ 799

9. 354 ◯ 345   97 ◯ 97   18 ◯ 18

10. 463 ◯ 463   118 ◯ 108   75 ◯ 117

FS109045 • Math Activities

Nearest Ten

Round each number to the nearest ten.

38 is closer to 40 than to 30.

Then 38 rounded to the nearest ten is 40.

30 31 32 33 34 35 36 37 38 39 40

A. 32 _____   G. 46 _____   M. 21 _____

B. 16 _____   H. 67 _____   N. 44 _____

C. 58 _____   I. 12 _____   O. 63 _____

D. 29 _____   J. 71 _____   P. 92 _____

E. 87 _____   K. 36 _____   Q. 54 _____

F. 42 _____   L. 83 _____   R. 79 _____

FS109045 • Math Activities

Nearest Hundred

Round each number to the nearest hundred.

230 is closer to 200 than to 300.

Then 230 rounded to the nearest hundred is 200.

200 210 220 230 240 250 260 270 280 290 300

A. 123 _____   G. 525 _____   M. 260 _____

B. 481 _____   H. 913 _____   N. 407 _____

C. 740 _____   I. 330 _____   O. 869 _____

D. 207 _____   J. 195 _____   P. 777 _____

E. 580 _____   K. 801 _____   Q. 930 _____

F. 362 _____   L. 672 _____   R. 618 _____

FS109045 • Math Activities

Zoo Animals

Use the chart to answer the questions below.

Animal	Number at Zoo
Bears	7
Camels	4
Elephants	6
Giraffes	3
Gorillas	3
Kangaroos	7
Lions	8
Snakes	12
Tigers	9
Zebras	10

A. How many elephants live at the zoo? _____

B. How many snakes live at the zoo? _____

C. How many more zebras than camels live at the zoo?

_____

D. Are there more lions or tigers at the zoo? _____

E. If the zoo got 3 more kangaroos, how many kangaroos would

there be in all? _____

FS109045 • Math Activities

Reptile House

Use the chart to answer the questions below about animals in the reptile house.

Reptile	Number at Zoo
Crocodiles	3
Lizards	6
Pythons	2
Rattlesnakes	4
Tortoises	8

A. How many lizards live at the zoo? _____

B. How many tortoises live at the zoo? _____

C. Are there more crocodiles or rattlesnakes at the zoo?

_____

D. How many more lizards than pythons are at the zoo?

_____

E. How many more tortoises than crocodiles are at the zoo?

_____

F. How many animals live in the reptile house in all? _____

Tuesday

Animal Parade

Look at the animal parade to answer the questions below.

A. Which animal is first? _____

B. Which animal is last? _____

C. Which animal is third? _____

D. Which animal is fourth? _____

E. Which animal is fifth? _____

F. How many are ahead of the armadillo? _____

G. What place in the parade is next to last? _____

H. How many are behind the bear? _____

     FS109045 • Math Activities

Lion Line

Each lion is a different color. Read the clues to discover the lions' colors. Then, color them.

1. The **orange** lion is fourth from the top.

2. The **brown** lion is farthest from the top.

3. The **yellow** lion is between the **orange** lion and the **brown** lion.

4. The **green** lion is four places above the **yellow** lion.

5. The **red** lion is right below the **green** lion.

6. The **blue** lion is beneath the **red** lion and above the **orange** lion.

FS109045 • Math Activities

Home Sweet Home

Add the numbers going across each box. Then add the numbers going down.

Den

12	+	18	=	
+	🐻	+	🐻	+
19	+	17	=	
=	🐻	=	🐻	=
	+		=	

Water

21	+	29	=	
+	🐟	+	🐟	+
19	+	13	=	
=	🐟	=	🐟	=
	+		=	

Jungle

34	+	27	=	
+	🐵	+	🐵	+
18	+	15	=	
=	🐵	=	🐵	=
	+		=	

Nest

26	+	24	=	
+	🐦	+	🐦	+
21	+	29	=	
=	🐦	=	🐦	=
	+		=	

Tree

13	+	26	=	
+	🐿️	+	🐿️	+
27	+	18	=	
=	🐿️	=	🐿️	=
	+		=	

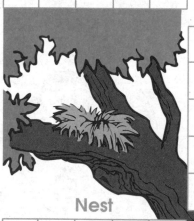

FS109045 • Math Activities

Turtle Path

Make a path for the turtle to the pond. Solve each problem. Then go back to start and shade each box whose difference has the numeral 3 or 4 in it.

start

74 − 38	46 − 23	40 − 23	82 − 64	25 − 17	57 − 29
35 − 17	93 − 56	72 − 28	92 − 24	56 − 37	93 − 17
47 − 29	65 − 38	82 − 46	56 − 17	88 − 59	38 − 29
27 − 19	42 − 16	35 − 29	61 − 47	85 − 17	67 − 39
74 − 48	93 − 25	63 − 36	82 − 29	36 − 17	53 − 27
43 − 26	74 − 46	50 − 25	82 − 69	61 − 18	53 − 16

FS109045 • Math Activities

Zoo Favorites

To find out what children like about the zoo, first solve the problems. Then, write the letter from the box whose answer matches the number below.

| 708 | 434 | 730 | 282 | 683 | 472 | 105 | 672 | 127 | 495 | ! |

R	563 − 281	I	378 + 294	E	868 − 138	T	767 − 295
G	718 − 223	E	523 + 185	N	396 − 269	Y	266 + 417
H	368 − 263	V	680 − 246				

FS109045 • Math Activities

What Time Is It?

To find out what time it is, solve each problem. Write the correct letter from the code box under each difference or sum.

3,768	92	2,615	1,073	1,873	5,114	4,037	5,468	5,956	1,560	185
I	L	T	N	E	U	M	O	G	H	C

4,321 − 1,706	1,972 + 1,796	5,500 − 1,463	7,361 − 5,488

1,546 + 1,069	9,016 − 3,548		3,082 + 2,874	2,781 + 2,687

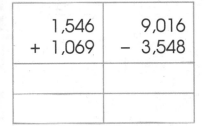
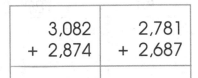

3,663 + 2,293	1,006 + 867	2,199 + 416

8,743 − 8,651	1,150 + 3,964	3,072 − 1,999	4,860 − 4,675	573 + 987

FS109045 • Math Activities

Llama's Mama

Add or subtract. Color the spaces with even answers in order from least to greatest to help the llama find its mama.

69 + 15	86 + 36	72 + 33

247 − 27	112 + 84	367 − 189	148 + 16	309 − 120
944 − 628	1,431 − 916	3,483 + 86	5,327 − 4,602	4,412 − 931
1,432 + 66	8,352 − 6,246	1,487 + 2,365		

FS109045 • Math Activities

Favorite Animals

Which animals have the most visitors at the zoo? To find out, match the answer for each problem to a letter in the box. Write the letter in the circle. Unscramble the letters in each row to name an animal.

L	127
P	101
G	2,488
R	28
E	47
I	326
H	761
N	152
T	141
A	1,809

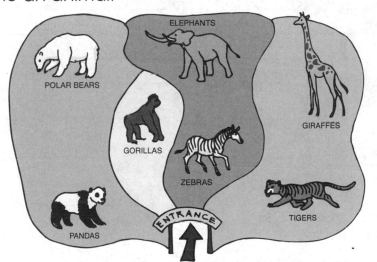

```
  124      9,048      43      174      3,562      83        37       143
+  28    - 7,239    +  4    - 127    - 2,801    + 58      + 64     -  16
```

◯ ◯ ◯ ◯ ◯ ◯ ◯ ◯

```
  3,825      159       26       282       961
- 1,337    - 131     + 21     +  44     - 820
```

◯ ◯ ◯ ◯ ◯

FS109045 • Math Activities

Busy Rhinos

The graph below shows what the rhinos in the
rhino pen are doing. Use the information in
the graph to answer the questions below.

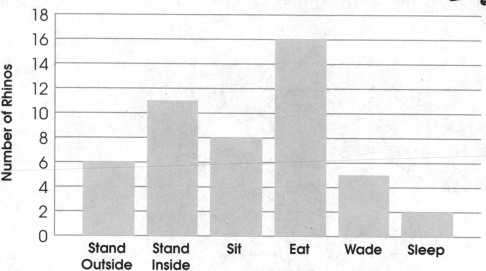

A. How many rhinos are wading in the water? _____

B. What are most rhinos doing? _____

C. How many are standing inside? _____

D. How many are standing inside and outside altogether?

   _____

E. How many more rhinos are sitting than wading? _____

F. What are the least amount of rhinos doing? _____

G. How many more rhinos are eating than sleeping? _____

H. If the 8 rhinos sitting down fall asleep, how many rhinos will be

   sleeping in all? _____

Which Way?

The number pair (1,8) gives you the location of the monkey. The first number tells you to go 1 space to the right (→). The second number tells you to go 8 spaces up (↑).

Use the graph to locate each animal at the zoo. Write the number pair for each animal.

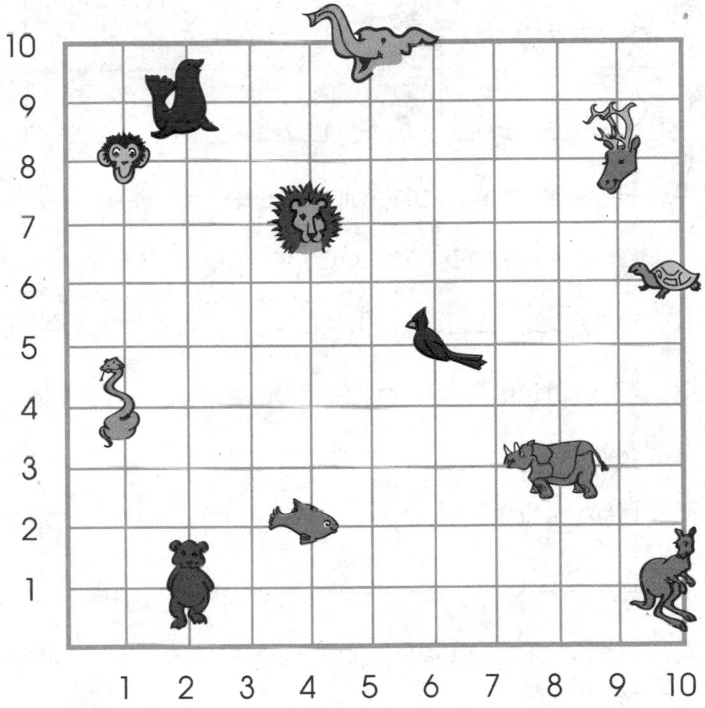

Reindeer _____

Kangaroo _____

Lion _____

Snake _____

Sea lion _____

Turtle _____

Fish _____

Bear _____

Elephant _____

Rhino _____

Bird _____

Welcome, Penguins!

Use the pictograph to answer each question below.

Penguins Delivered to Zoo

Monday	🐧 🐧
Tuesday	🐧 🐧 🐧 🐧
Wednesday	🐧 🐧 🐧
Thursday	🐧
Friday	🐧 🐧

🐧 = 2 penguins

A. How many penguins were delivered to the zoo on Thursday? _____

B. On what two days did the zoo receive the same amount of penguins? _____

_____

C. How many penguins were delivered on Tuesday?

_____

D. On what day were the fewest penguins delivered to the zoo? _____

E. On what day were the most penguins delivered to the zoo? _____

F. How many penguins were delivered on Thursday and Friday altogether? _____

G. How many more penguins were delivered on Tuesday than on Monday? _____

H. How many penguins in all were delivered to the zoo this week? _____

30   FS109045 • Math Activities

Penguin's Busy Day

Use the table to answer each question below.

Penguin Schedule					
Breakfast	7:00 a.m.	**Lunch**	11:15 a.m.	**Dinner**	4:30 p.m.
Playtime	7:45 a.m.	**Nap**	12:00 noon	**Showtime**	6:00 p.m.
Snack	9:00 a.m.	**Playtime**	3:20 p.m.	**Bath**	7:40 p.m.
Showtime	9:30 a.m.			**Bedtime**	8:10 p.m.

A. At what time do the penguins eat breakfast? _____

B. What do the penguins do before morning showtime? _____

C. At what times do the penguins play? _____ and

_____

D. How many times do the penguins eat each day? _____

E. How many shows do the penguins do each day? _____

F. At what times do the penguins sleep each day?

_____ and _____

Check the Times

Write the time shown on the clock below each activity.

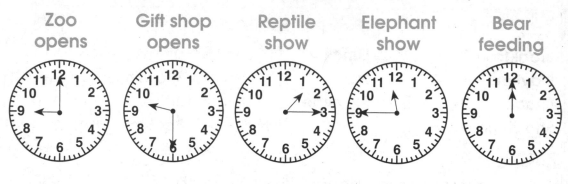

Zoo opens	Gift shop opens	Reptile show	Elephant show	Bear feeding
__ __ : __ __	__ __ : __ __	__ __ : __ __	__ __ : __ __	__ __ : __ __

Draw the hands on the clocks.

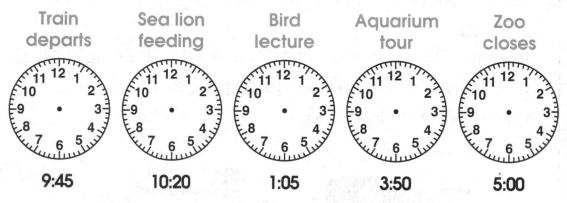

Train departs	Sea lion feeding	Bird lecture	Aquarium tour	Zoo closes
9:45	10:20	1:05	3:50	5:00

FS109045 • Math Activities

Early or Late?

Compare pairs of clocks to determine if the zookeeper is early or late. Then write the amount of time the zookeeper is early or late.

Time to Start	Zookeeper Arrives	Early or Late? (Circle)
![clock] _____	![clock] _____	Early Late _____ hours _____ minutes
![clock] _____	![clock] _____	Early Late _____ hours _____ minutes
![clock] _____	![clock] _____	Early Late _____ hours _____ minutes
![clock] _____	![clock] _____	Early Late _____ hours _____ minutes
![clock] _____	![clock] _____	Early Late _____ hours _____ minutes

FS109045 • Math Activities

Visiting the Gift Shop

Write the number of each coin needed to make the exact change. Use the least possible number of coins.

66¢ 23¢ 37¢ 60¢
49¢ 38¢ 96¢ 55¢

A. Jamal wants to buy a .	1	1	0	3
B. Kelly wants to buy a .				
C. Gilberto wants to buy a .				
D. Maria wants to buy a .				
E. Todd wants to buy a .				

FS109045 • Math Activities

Thank You, Come Again!

For each purchase, find the amount of change received and write it in the box.

Item Purchased	Money Given to Clerk	Change Received
96¢ (turtle)	$1.00	
37¢ (seal)	75¢	
28¢ (eel)	50¢	
57¢ (tadpole)	$1.00	
55¢ (lizard)	$1.00	
72¢ (llama)	$1.00	
66¢ (kangaroo)	$5.00	
66¢, 66¢ (kangaroo and octopus)	$5.00	

FS109045 • Math Activities

Monkey Business

Label the shapes.

circle
cone
sphere
triangle
cube
square
cylinder
rectangle

1. _____

2. _____

3. _____

4. _____

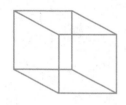

5. _____

6. _____

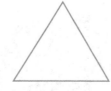

7. _____

8. _____

FS109045 • Math Activities

Fraction Fun

Look at the shapes. Write a fraction to show how many parts of each shape are shaded.

A.

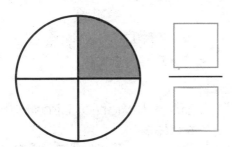

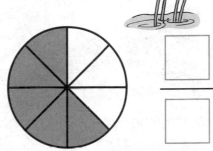

B.

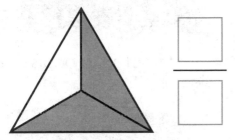

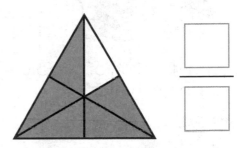

C.

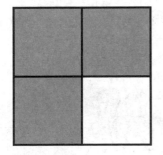

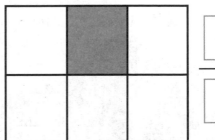

FS109045 • Math Activities

How Many?

Look at each picture. Write a fraction that answers each question.

A. What fraction of the frogs are on the lily pad?

E. What fraction of fish are striped?

B. What fraction of the monkeys are eating bananas?

F. What fraction of birds are in the tree?

C. What fraction of alligators are in the water?

G. What fraction of bears are sleeping?

D. What fraction of lions are cubs?

H. What fraction of horses are standing?

FS109045 • Math Activities

Silly Shapes

Look at each row. Write the fraction that shows how much is shaded in the first picture. Then shade parts of the other picture to make an equivalent fraction.

A.    is equal to

B.    is equal to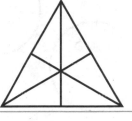

C.    is equal to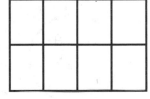

D.    is equal to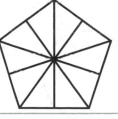

E.    is equal to

     FS109045 • Math Activities

Bouncing Balls

Solve each problem.

$$\begin{array}{r} 5 \\ \times\ 4 \\ \hline \end{array}$$

$$\begin{array}{r} 5 \\ \times\ 8 \\ \hline \end{array}$$

$$\begin{array}{r} 3 \\ \times\ 3 \\ \hline \end{array}$$

$$\begin{array}{r} 6 \\ \times\ 1 \\ \hline \end{array}$$

$$\begin{array}{r} 7 \\ \times\ 2 \\ \hline \end{array}$$

$$\begin{array}{r} 2 \\ \times\ 9 \\ \hline \end{array}$$

$$\begin{array}{r} 4 \\ \times\ 7 \\ \hline \end{array}$$

$$\begin{array}{r} 8 \\ \times\ 7 \\ \hline \end{array}$$

$$\begin{array}{r} 6 \\ \times\ 3 \\ \hline \end{array}$$

$$\begin{array}{r} 1 \\ \times\ 7 \\ \hline \end{array}$$

$$\begin{array}{r} 2 \\ \times\ 6 \\ \hline \end{array}$$

$$\begin{array}{r} 4 \\ \times\ 9 \\ \hline \end{array}$$

$$\begin{array}{r} 6 \\ \times\ 5 \\ \hline \end{array}$$

$$\begin{array}{r} 8 \\ \times\ 3 \\ \hline \end{array}$$

$$\begin{array}{r} 5 \\ \times\ 8 \\ \hline \end{array}$$

$$\begin{array}{r} 9 \\ \times\ 3 \\ \hline \end{array}$$

$$\begin{array}{r} 3 \\ \times\ 5 \\ \hline \end{array}$$

$$\begin{array}{r} 8 \\ \times\ 6 \\ \hline \end{array}$$

FS109045 • Math Activities

The Largest Zoo

Solve each problem. Use the code to find the name of the largest zoo in tho world.

A	D	E	G	I	K	L	M	N	O	P	R	S	W
36	12	56	27	24	45	16	42	18	21	30	54	15	81

$$\begin{array}{cc} 3 \\ \times\ 5 \end{array} \quad \begin{array}{cc} 6 \\ \times\ 6 \end{array} \quad \begin{array}{cc} 9 \\ \times\ 2 \end{array} \qquad \begin{array}{cc} 6 \\ \times\ 2 \end{array} \quad \begin{array}{cc} 2 \\ \times\ 12 \end{array} \quad \begin{array}{cc} 8 \\ \times\ 7 \end{array} \quad \begin{array}{cc} 3 \\ \times\ 9 \end{array} \quad \begin{array}{cc} 7 \\ \times\ 3 \end{array}$$

□ □ □   □ □ □ □ □

$$\begin{array}{cc} 9 \\ \times\ 9 \end{array} \quad \begin{array}{cc} 8 \\ \times\ 3 \end{array} \quad \begin{array}{cc} 2 \\ \times\ 8 \end{array} \quad \begin{array}{cc} 3 \\ \times\ 4 \end{array} \qquad \begin{array}{cc} 9 \\ \times\ 4 \end{array} \quad \begin{array}{cc} 6 \\ \times\ 3 \end{array} \quad \begin{array}{cc} 4 \\ \times\ 6 \end{array} \quad \begin{array}{cc} 6 \\ \times\ 7 \end{array} \quad \begin{array}{cc} 12 \\ \times\ 3 \end{array} \quad \begin{array}{cc} 4 \\ \times\ 4 \end{array}$$

□ □ □ □   □ □ □ □ □ □

$$\begin{array}{cc} 10 \\ \times\ 3 \end{array} \quad \begin{array}{cc} 3 \\ \times\ 12 \end{array} \quad \begin{array}{cc} 9 \\ \times\ 6 \end{array} \quad \begin{array}{cc} 9 \\ \times\ 5 \end{array}$$

□ □ □ □

FS109045 • Math Activities

Bear Facts

Complete the charts below.

x	2	1	7
3			
5			
1			

x	1	0	5
8			
9			
7			

x	5	6	2
8			
1			
4			

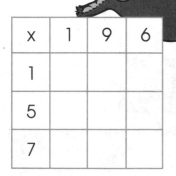

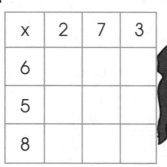

x	2	7	3
6			
5			
8			

x	4	0	3
3			
1			
8			

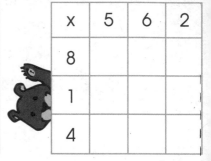

x	1	9	6
1			
5			
7			

x	9	2	6
5			
3			
2			

x	1	2	3
5			
8			
2			

FS109045 • Math Activities

Dividing Them Up

Complete each division chart.

÷ 2	
14	
8	
20	
4	

÷ 7	
49	
21	
63	
56	

÷ 9	
18	
63	
36	
72	

÷ 4	
12	
4	
36	
28	

÷ 5	
35	
50	
15	
20	

÷ 8	
32	
24	
40	
72	

÷ 3	
18	
6	
27	
9	

÷ 6	
18	
36	
54	
48	

43

FS109045 • Math Activities

Bear Fact Families

Use the numbers on each bear family to write a fact family.

____ X ____ = ____

____ X ____ = ____

____ ÷ ____ = ____

____ ÷ ____ = ____

____ X ____ = ____

____ X ____ = ____

____ ÷ ____ = ____

____ ÷ ____ = ____

____ X ____ = ____

____ X ____ = ____

____ ÷ ____ = ____

____ ÷ ____ = ____

____ X ____ = ____

____ X ____ = ____

____ ÷ ____ = ____

____ ÷ ____ = ____

____ X ____ = ____

____ X ____ = ____

____ ÷ ____ = ____

____ ÷ ____ = ____

____ X ____ = ____

____ X ____ = ____

____ ÷ ____ = ____

____ ÷ ____ = ____

FS109045 • Math Activities

Feeding Time

Read each story problem. Multiply or divide to solve the problem.

A. The zookeeper feeds each sea lion 3 fish. There are 4 sea lions. How many fish does the zookeeper need?

_____

D. The zookeeper has 24 apples. There are 8 camels. How many apples will each camel get?

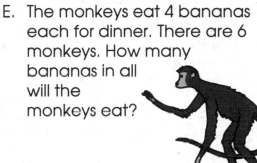

_____

B. There are 5 hungry frogs. Each frog eats 5 flies. How many flies do the frogs eat altogether?

_____

E. The monkeys eat 4 bananas each for dinner. There are 6 monkeys. How many bananas in all will the monkeys eat?

_____

C. The zookeeper has 30 peanuts. There are 6 elephants. How many peanuts will each elephant get?

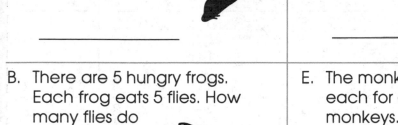

_____

F. It takes the zookeeper 8 minutes to feed each bear family. There are 7 bear families altogether. How long does it take the zookeeper to feed them all?

_____

Where Is Mother Bear?

To help the bear cub find its mother, fill in the missing number for each problem. If the missing number is 5, color the whole box.

8 9 × 4 3 ☐ 6	☐ 3 × 2 1 0 6	7 1 × 6 ☐ 2 6	1 2 × ☐ 3 6	3 7 × ☐ 2 5 9
2 ☐ × 6 1 6 2	2 2 × 8 1 ☐ 6	7 ☐ × 3 2 2 5	4 6 × ☐ 2 3 0	☐ 6 × 7 2 5 2	1 8 × ☐ 7 2
☐ 8 × 3 1 4 4	6 5 × ☐ 2 6 0	1 ☐ × 8 1 4 4	5 3 × 3 1 ☐ 9	6 ☐ × 4 2 4 8	3 3 × 6 1 9 ☐
5 6 × ☐ 5 0 4	2 5 × 6 1 ☐ 0	2 ☐ × 5 1 2 5	4 9 × 5 2 4 ☐	☐ 5 × 2 5 0	4 4 × 5 2 ☐ 0
4 2 × 6 2 ☐ 2	1 5 × 7 1 0 ☐	3 ☐ × 3 1 1 4	3 7 × 8 ☐ 9 6	☐ 6 × 3 1 0 8	1 9 × ☐ 1 7 1
7 ☐ × 2 1 5 0	☐ 8 × 4 1 9 2	5 ☐ × 5 2 8 0	☐ 2 × 8 3 3 6		
7 8 × 2 1 ☐ 6	8 9 × 4 3 ☐ 6	3 3 × ☐ 1 6 5	2 4 × ☐ 1 2 0		

FS109045 • Math Activities

All Kinds of Bears

To find the names of different kinds of bears at the zoo, solve the problems. Then use the answers and the code to write the names of the bears.

R	P	N	K	A	L	O	B	C	W
90	144	378	396	484	609	684	690	1,794	2,045

345 x 2	10 x 9	342 x 2	409 x 5	54 x 7

138 x 5	87 x 7	242 x 2	299 x 6	44 x 9

36 x 4	171 x 4	203 x 3	121 x 4	18 x 5

FS109045 • Math Activities

Panda Path

Solve each problem. Color the squares with even answers in order to make a path from the panda to the bamboo shoots.

	$5\overline{)70}$	$3\overline{)57}$	$4\overline{)52}$
$2\overline{)86}$	$3\overline{)84}$	$2\overline{)58}$	$5\overline{)455}$
$7\overline{)112}$	$3\overline{)96}$	$3\overline{)99}$	$4\overline{)236}$
$2\overline{)108}$	$3\overline{)129}$	$6\overline{)210}$	$7\overline{)455}$
$5\overline{)330}$	$3\overline{)204}$	$5\overline{)210}$	

FS109045 • Math Activities

Turtle Trail

Solve each problem. Use the code to color each turtle.

$9 \overline{)31}$ $8 \overline{)44}$ $6 \overline{)52}$

$4 \overline{)26}$ $5 \overline{)24}$ $3 \overline{)41}$

$7 \overline{)64}$ $8 \overline{)76}$ $9 \overline{)37}$

Remainder	1	2	4
Color	red	yellow	green

Slithering Serpent

Solve each problem to help the snake get back to its cage.

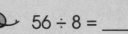

$56 \div 8 =$ _____

$28 \div 7 =$ _____

$9 \times 2 =$ _____

$5 \times 7 =$ _____

$36 \div 6 =$ _____

$15 \div 3 =$ _____

$8 \times 3 =$ _____

$6 \times 5 =$ _____

$10 \div 2 =$ _____

$63 \div 9 =$ _____

$12 \times 4 =$ _____

$24 \div 3 =$ _____

$7 \times 7 =$ _____

FS109045 • Math Activities

Zoo Friends

Solve the problems from left to right. Then, use the answers to color the graph.

A. $4 \times 3 =$ _____ $\times 5 =$ _____ $\div 3 =$

B. $7 \times 6 =$ _____ $- 2 =$ _____ $\div 4 =$

C. $64 \div 8 =$ _____ $- 3 =$ _____ $\times 5 =$

D. $36 \div 6 =$ _____ $\div 2 =$ _____ $\times 10 =$

E. $5 \times 5 =$ _____ $+ 5 =$ _____ $\div 6 =$

FS109045 • Math Activities

Page 2

8 + 2 =	6 + 6 =	4 + 4 =	5 + 8 =
10	**12**	**8**	**13**
11 + 6 =	13 + 4 =	10 + 6 =	13 + 2 =
17	**17**	**16**	**15**

7 + 6 =	11 + 2 =	3 + 3 =	8 + 4 =	7 + 7 =	5 + 11 =	14 + 5 =
13	**13**	**6**	**12**	**14**	**16**	**19**
8 + 7 =	4 + 9 =	5 + 7 =	12 + 5 =	10 + 5 =	9 + 8 =	9 + 4 =
15	**13**	**12**	**17**	**15**	**17**	**13**
11 + 3 =	12 + 6 =	9 + 7 =	15 + 4 =	12 + 3 =	17 + 4 =	7 + 10 =
14	**18**	**16**	**19**	**15**	**21**	**17**
7 + 5 =	5 + 12 =	9 + 4 =	4 + 7 =	9 + 6 =	6 + 7 =	8 + 5 =
12	**17**	**13**	**11**	**15**	**13**	**13**
6 + 8 =	4 + 6 =	2 + 12 =	8 + 5 =	15 + 2 =		
14	**10**	**14**	**13**	**17**		
15 + 2 =	7 + 8 =	5 + 9 =	4 + 8 =	6 + 8 =		
17	**15**	**14**	**12**	**14**		

Page 3
1. 8, 2, 4, 8, 12, 10
2. 2, 6, 13, 5, 13, 14
3. 8, 7, 9, 3, 1, 7
4. 12, 2, 4, 6, 2, 14
5. 6, 20, 13, 8

Page 4
1. 10; 7; 12; 9; 13; frogs
2. 8; 7; 12; 8; 12; 5; 11; 4; 6; 13; crocodiles
3. 10; 11; 13; 14; fish

Page 5
1. The number is 4.
   9 + 4 = 13
   4 + 9 = 13
   13 – 9 = 4
   13 – 4 = 9
2. The number is 8.
   7 + 8 = 15
   8 + 7 = 15
   15 – 8 = 7
   15 – 7 = 8
3. The number is 12.
   3 + 9 = 12
   9 + 3 = 12
   12 – 9 = 3
   12 – 3 = 9

4. The number is 6.
   3 + 6 = 9
   6 + 3 = 9
   9 – 3 = 6
   9 – 6 = 3

Page 6
1. 12, 12, 11, 12
2. 14, 14, 14, 15
3. 17, 18, 17, 17
4. 13, 13, 14, 13

Page 7

5	0	7
6	**4**	**2**
1	8	**3**

10	**5**	**6**
3	7	**11**
8	**9**	**4**

2	**9**	4
7	**5**	**3**
6	1	**8**

Page 8
A. 18 – 5 = 13 snakes
B. 9 – 6 = 3 turtles
C. 8 + 9 = 17 lizards
D. 4 + 12 = 16 alligators and fish

Page 9
8, 20
9, 13
3, check student problem

Page 10
Frisky - 237
Rex - 345
Whiskers - 430
Scratch - 383
Claude - 204
First place - Whiskers
Second place - Scratch
Third place - Rex
Fourth place - Frisky
Fifth place - Claude

Page 11

Page 12
1. 24
2. 509
3. 1,071
4. 100
5. 8,605
6. 222
7. 7,649
8. 330
9. 50
10. 822

Page 13
A. 3
B. 3
C. snake
D. 1
E. snake, zebra, tiger
F. turtle, alligator, snake

Page 14
1. >, <, <
2. >, >, >
3. <, =, <
4. >, >, >
5. <, <, =

Page 15
1. =, =, <
2. =, <, >
3. <, >, =
4. =, =, <
5. >, >, <
6. >, =, <
7. =, <, >
8. <, <, >
9. >, =, =
10. =, >, <

Page 16
A. 30	G. 50	M. 20
B. 20	H. 70	N. 40
C. 60	I. 10	O. 60
D. 30	J. 70	P. 90
E. 90	K. 40	Q. 50
F. 40	L. 80	R. 80

Page 17
A. 100	G. 500	M. 300
B. 500	H. 900	N. 400
C. 700	I. 300	O. 900
D. 200	J. 200	P. 800
E. 600	K. 800	Q. 900
F. 400	L. 700	R. 600

Page 18
A. 6
B. 12
C. 6
D. tigers
E. 10

Page 19
A. 6
B. 8
C. rattlesnakes
D. 4
E. 5
F. 23

Page 20
A. giraffe
B. monkey
C. bear
D. snake
E. parrot
F. 5
G. 6th
H. 4

Page 21
1st lion—green
2nd lion—red
3rd lion—blue
4th lion—orange
5th lion—yellow
6th lion—brown

Page 22
Den

12	+	18	=	**30**
+		+		+
19	+	17	=	**36**
=		=		=
31	+	**35**	=	**66**

Water

21	+	29	=	**50**
+		+		+
19	+	13	=	**32**
=		=		-
40	+	**42**	=	**82**

Jungle

34	+	27	=	**61**
+		+		+
18	+	15	=	**33**
-		=		=
52	+	**42**	=	**94**

Nest

26	+	24	=	**50**
+		+		+
21	+	29	=	**50**
=		=		=
47	+	**53**	=	**100**

Tree

13	+	26	=	**39**
+		+		+
27	+	18	=	**45**
=		=		=
40	+	**44**	=	**84**

Page 23
74 − 38 **36**	46 − 23 **23**	40 − 23 **17**	82 − 64 **18**	25 − 17 **8**	57 − 29 **28**
35 − 17 **18**	93 − 56 **37**	72 − 28 **44**	92 − 24 **68**	56 − 37 **19**	93 − 17 **76**
47 − 29 **18**	65 − 38 **27**	82 − 46 **36**	56 − 17 **39**	88 − 59 **29**	38 − 29 **9**
27 − 19 **8**	42 − 16 **26**	35 − 29 **6**	61 47 **14**	85 − 17 **68**	67 − 39 **28**
74 − 48 **26**	93 − 25 **68**	63 − 36 **27**	82 − 29 **53**	36 − 17 **19**	53 − 27 **26**
43 − 26 **17**	74 − 46 **28**	50 − 25 **25**	82 − 69 **13**	61 − 18 **43**	53 − 16 **37**

Page 24
EVERYTHING!

R 563 − 281 **282**	I 378 + 294 **672**	E 868 − 138 **730**	I 767 − 295 **472**
G 718 − 223 **495**	E 523 + 185 **708**	N 396 − 269 **127**	Y 266 + 417 **683**
H 368 − 263 **105**	V 680 − 246 **434**		

Page 25
2,615; 3,768; 4,037; 1,873
2,615, 5,468; 5,956; 5,468
5,956; 1,873; 2,615
92; 5,114; 1,073; 185; 1,560
TIME TO GO GET LUNCH

Page 26

		69 + 15 **84**	86 + 36 **122**	72 + 33 **105**
247 − 27 **220**	112 + 84 **196**	367 − 189 **178**	148 + 16 **164**	309 − 120 **189**
944 − 628 **316**	1,431 − 916 **515**	3,483 + 86 **3,569**	5,327 − 4,602 **725**	4,412 − 931 **3,481**
1,432 + 66 **1,498**	8,352 − 6,246 **2,106**	1,487 + 2,365 **3,852**		

Page 27
152; 1,809; 47; 47; 761;
141; 101; 127; elephant
2; 888; 28; 47; 326; 141;
tiger

Page 28
A. 5
B. eating
C. 11
D. 17
E. 3
F. sleeping
G. 14
H. 10

Page 29
reindeer—(9,8)
kangaroo—(10, 1)
lion—(4, 7)
snake—(1, 4)
sea lion—(2, 9)
turtle—(10, 6)
fish—(4, 2)
bear—(2, 1)
elephant—(5, 10)
rhino—(8, 3)
bird—(6, 5)

Page 30
A. 2
B. Monday, Friday
C. 8
D. Thursday
E. Tuesday
F. 6
G. 4
H. 24

Page 31
A. 7:00 a.m.
B. snack
C. 7:45 a.m., 3:20 p.m.
D. 4
E. 2
F. 12:00 noon, 8:10 p.m.

Page 32
9:00, 9:30, 1:15, 11:45, 12:00

Page 33
10:00, 9:30, early, 30 minutes
2:00, 11:30, early, 2 hours 30
    minutes
11:45, 12:05, late, 20 minutes
3:20, 3:30, late, 10 minutes
4:00, 5:05, late, 1 hour
    5 minutes

Page 34

1	1	0	3
1	2	0	4
0	2	0	3
1	1	0	2
2	0	1	0

Page 35
4¢
38¢
22¢
43¢
45¢
28¢
$4.34
$3.68

Page 36
1. square   2. cone
3. cylinder   4. rectangle
5. cube   6. sphere
7. circle   8. triangle

Page 37
A. ¼, ⅝
B. ⅔, ⅚
C. ¾, ⅙

Page 38
A. ¼   E. ²⁄₇
B. ⅔   F. ⁹⁄₁₀
C. ¾   G. ⁵⁄₇
D. ⅚   H. ⅝

Page 39

A. $\frac{1}{2}$ is equal to

B. $\frac{1}{3}$ is equal to

C. $\frac{1}{4}$ is equal to

D. $\frac{2}{5}$ is equal to

E. $\frac{3}{4}$ is equal to

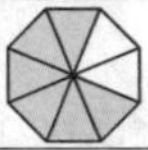

Page 40

Page 41
15, 36, 18; 12, 24, 56, 27, 21;
81, 24, 16, 12; 36, 18, 24, 42,
36, 16; 30, 36, 54, 45
SAN DIEGO WILD ANIMAL
PARK

Page 42

x	2	1	7
3	6	3	21
5	10	15	35
1	2	1	7

x	1	0	5
8	8	0	40
9	9	0	45
7	7	0	35

x	5	6	2
8	40	48	16
1	5	6	2
4	20	24	8

x	2	7	3
6	12	42	18
5	10	35	15
8	16	56	24

x	4	0	3
3	12	0	9
1	4	0	3
8	32	0	24

x	1	9	6
1	1	9	6
5	5	45	30
7	7	63	42

x	9	2	6
5	45	10	30
3	27	6	18
2	18	4	12

x	1	2	3
5	5	10	15
8	8	16	24
2	2	4	6

Page 43

÷2	
14	7
8	4
20	10
4	2

÷7	
49	7
21	3
63	9
56	8

÷9	
18	2
63	7
36	4
72	8

÷4	
12	3
4	1
36	9
28	7

÷5	
35	7
50	10
15	3
20	4

÷8	
32	4
24	3
40	5
72	9

÷3	
18	6
6	2
27	9
9	3

÷6	
18	3
36	6
54	9
48	8

Page 44

3 x 7 = 21	3 x 4 = 12
7 x 3 = 21	4 x 3 = 12
21 ÷ 3 = 7	12 ÷ 3 = 4
21 ÷ 7 = 3	12 ÷ 4 = 3
6 x 9 = 54	5 x 7 = 35
9 x 6 = 54	7 x 5 = 35
54 ÷ 6 = 9	35 ÷ 5 = 7
54 ÷ 9 = 6	35 ÷ 7 = 5
3 x 10 = 30	4 x 8 = 32
10 x 3 = 30	8 x 4 = 32
30 ÷ 3 = 10	32 ÷ 4 = 8
30 ÷ 10 = 3	32 ÷ 8 = 4

Page 45

A. 3 x 4 = 12 fish
B. 5 x 5 = 25 flies
C. 30 ÷ 6 = 5 peanuts
D. 24 ÷ 8 = 3 apples
E. 6 x 4 = 24 bananas
F. 8 x 7 = 56 minutes

Page 46

89 x4 = 356	53 x2 = 106	71 x6 = 426	12 x3 = 36	37 x7 = 259
27 x6 = 162	22 x8 = 176	75 x3 = 225	46 x5 = 230	36 x7 = 252	18 x4 = 72
48 x3 = 144	65 x4 = 260	18 x8 = 144	53 x3 = 159	62 x4 = 248	33 x6 = 198
56 x9 = 504	25 x6 = 150	25 x5 = 125	49 x5 = 245	25 x2 = 50	44 x5 = 220
42 x6 = 252	15 x7 = 105	38 x3 = 114	37 x8 = 296	36 x3 = 108	19 x9 = 171
75 x2 = 150	48 x4 = 192	56 x5 = 280	42 x8 = 336		
78 x2 = 156	89 x4 = 356	33 x5 = 165	24 x5 = 120		

Page 47

690, 90, 684, 2,045, 378
BROWN
690, 609, 484, 1,794, 396
BLACK
144, 684, 609, 484, 90
POLAR

Page 48

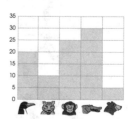

14 5)70	19 3)57	13 4)52
43 2)86	28 3)84	29 2)58	91 5)455
16 7)112	32 3)96	33 3)99	59 4)236
54 2)108	43 3)129	35 6)210	65 7)455
66 5)330	68 3)204	42 5)210	

Page 49

9)31 3r4   8)44 5r4   6)52 8r4

4)26 6r2   5)24 4r4   3)41 13r2

7)64 9r1   8)76 9r4   9)37 4r1

Page 50

7
4
18
35
6
5
24
30
5
7
48
8
49

Page 51

A. 12, 60, 20
B. 42, 40, 10
C. 8, 5, 25
D. 6, 3, 30
E. 25, 30, 5

    FS109045 • Math Activities

_____
is super smart in math!

Great job!

_____
signature

_____
date